HOW TO WRITE A HAIKU

Also by David Lindley

Essays
The Freedom to be Tragic
Ideas of Order

Poetry and translations
The Song of Myself: a new verse translation of The Bhagavad Gita
Something and Nothing: Selected Poems
Book of Days

First published 2016 by Verborum Editions

www.verborumeditions.com

978-1-907100-05-5

HOW TO WRITE A HAIKU

by
David Lindley

Verborum Editions

CONTENTS

HOW TO WRITE A HAIKU

The poet gives this moment, and that is all. Karl Shapiro

No ideas but in things. William Carlos Williams

I love this old Bashō tree for its uselessness. I sit under it, and enjoy the wind and rain blowing against it. Matsuo Bashō

What is a haiku?

Anyone reading a Japanese haiku, either in the original language or in translation, will immediately become aware of its salient features: its *brevity*, by being limited to a total of 17 *syllables*; its *form* of three lines of 5, 7 and 5 syllables; the concreteness of its *images* (trees, flowers, blossom, water, wind, leaves, insects, birds); and how it *suggests*, rather than states, a mood, a feeling, an emotional response to a particular experience purely by the conjunction of words and the juxtaposition of images. Haiku, in brief, seem to capture the significant moment in its passing. They might adequately be defined as 'records of high moments'.[1]

If the successful haiku speaks for itself, without the need for further elaboration by the poet or an explanation demanded by the reader, then the above description of the haiku will serve to sum up all we need to know about it. The more we say, the farther away from the essence of the haiku we find ourselves. Yet, if we wish to capture our own fleeting experiences, our 'high moments', in the form of the haiku we must look further into how the haiku achieves

[1] Harold G Henderson, *An Introduction to Haiku.* New York, Doubleday. 1958

its effect. In doing so, since we shall be looking at the creation of haiku in English, we shall be asking a few questions about the history and origins of this particular verse form in Japanese culture, and the extent to which that tradition is transferable to the English language.

Let us look first at an example of a classical Japanese haiku to note some of the points we will be discussing. This is a famous early haiku by the best known of all haiku masters, Matsuo Bashō (1644-1694):

On a withered branch
crows are settling down to roost.
Autumn, night falling.[1]

Here is a transcription of the haiku in Japanese:

kare-eda ni
karasu no tomari-keri
aki no kure

Technically, there are three lines of 5, 7 and 5 syllables with a break between the first two lines and the third — indicated in the English version by a period, in the Japanese by the suffix *-keri*, which is a stylised way of ending a completed thought or image and here has no syllabic value. It divides the haiku into two complementary parts, with each dependent on the other for the overall effect of creating a particular mood. The crows have come down to settle on a bare branch. There is in the opening lines a sense not only of the day closing, but of the day's activity

---

[1] All translations are by the author

coming to an end and, in the final line, of the year itself ending. A falling, a decline, an ending – all summoning up an inner feeling of loneliness or lateness suggested, but not explicitly stated, by an association of images. If we take time to dwell on these images, we will find greater depths of association as we think also of leaves falling or having already fallen, of what we wished for that has not been accomplished, of the passing of time, or perhaps of resting, reflecting, accepting...

We may need to read a haiku over and over again, or learn it by heart, to grasp the full depth of its meaning and associations. Reading haiku is just as much an art as writing them. Since it *is* an art, like all art it has its technical aspects, just like painting or photography or even simply the art of cultivating a state of mindfulness where we do not let the moment pass unnoticed or unobserved – without which there would be no art of painting or photography or poetry. It follows, therefore, that in writing a haiku it is not enough, on the one hand, simply to pick out a number of 'poetic' images and link them together to make a sort of appreciative statement:

I love hearing birds
calling under my window.
Early morning mist.

Or, on the other hand, to rattle off a few words about some inconsequential personal event as though it were a 'high moment'. Here is one I found among the many thousands of 'haiku' published on the internet:

I picked up
my cell phone
and said 'Hi.'

Observation, thoughtfulness, discrimination and a certain amount of effort are required to master the art of haiku, which in themselves, when they are successful, look deceptively simple. Some haiku do indeed look very superficial (and some probably are), but their surfaces, like an old pond, have great depths under them.

The origins of haiku

The haiku did not make its appearance as a verse form in its own right until the 17th century. The 'longer' form that preceded it, the *tanka* or *uta*, a short verse or 'song' of 31 syllables, is made up of a stanza of five lines with the syllabic pattern 5,7,5,7,7. These verses could be linked together to make longer verse sequences but they never became what we would recognise as 'long' poems. Traditional Japanese poetry does not attempt to sustain a narrative or exhaust an idea or develop a metaphor or a poetic 'fancy'. What is captured in one five-line unit of verse sets (usually quite formally) the starting point, by association (whether with reference to an earlier well known poem, a seasonal image or word, or something in the mind of the poet) for the next verse.

There is nothing revolutionary to be found in the history of Japanese versification, though it has its own subtle evolution from aristocratic beginnings and, as one might expect of a tradition spanning many centuries, poetic diction changed, following a bumpy road from strict formality of expression to a more demotic and colloquial style.

One of the most famous collections of Japanese traditional verse (from around the year 759) is the *Man'yōshū*, a remarkable anthology of all that was considered worth preserving from the earliest ages of Japanese poetry, and it remains an inspiring source for later traditions. The poems cover a wide variety of topics from folksongs to laments, love poetry and reflections on nature, and were written by emperors and princes, frontier guards, herbalists, clerks, priests, women and girls. However, in the centuries that followed, poetry became an activity carried on principally by nobles and courtiers; the writing of verse was a highly valued demonstration of a refined sensibility befitting a member of the imperial court. There were rules for the writing of poems, just as there were codes for appropriate dress for various indoor and outdoor occasions, and none could be flouted in the name of self-expression.

The writing of verses was both an integral part of court etiquette and a stylised form of communication, an accomplishment to be expected of any lady or gentleman of rank. We can find many instances of this practice in the two most important classical prose works of the Heian period (when the imperial court was established in Kyoto), both dating from the 11th century. In the *Pillow Book of Sei Shōnagon*, for example, in one incident Sei Shōnagon is bored so sets off with some of her companions to hear the cuckoo, one of many seasonal acts of observance, like the viewing of cherry blossoms or the full moon, that comprise the Japanese aesthetic sensibility. When she gets back to court, the Empress asks to hear her poem on the cuckoo which she was expected to have written on the spot. But the somewhat distracted Sei Shōnagon hasn't written one, and now finds it too hard to think back to the occasion and write a poem 'recollected in tranquillity' (to quote Words-worth's theory and practice of poetry) and is censured for her failure by the Empress herself. In the long and complex *Tale of Genji*, the amorous Prince Genji brings forth a poem, or is 'reminded' of a poem, at each encounter with a flower in bloom or a new girl. And just as the poem produced on the spot is an essential aid to seduction, the spontaneous poem in response serves to objectify feelings not directly expressed in what would have been considered too frank an exchange, so that both the seducer and the seduced in effect immediately translate their desires into a highly stylised aesthetic experience.

The poem, as a form of expression of one's personal feelings in a world confined and constrained by sets of rules that governed behaviour and limited freedom of open interaction, became a discreet medium of communication between lovers – or, in that cloistered environment, between a noble of the court and the shadow of a lady behind a screen or shutter. The poem, shuffled from sleeve to sleeve, and the brushstrokes on paper that betrayed the hand (not forgetting the importance of the quality of the paper itself or its retained perfume) became the medium through which the affair was conducted and, indeed, in many instances, *was* the affair itself, an affair of longings and sighs.

The orthodox 31 syllable poem of five lines lent itself to the competitive demonstration of skill and aesthetic sensibility among accomplished poets at court, and that practice became a refined sort of parlour game that endured for many centuries, leading to the later classical linked verse sequences known as *renga*. One poet would write the opening three lines, with their own conclusion, and another complete the verse with the final two complementary lines. The next, or former, poet would take his cue from those two lines and write the next three-line sequence. In the one hundred verse sequence, the *Minase sangin hyakuin*, dating from 1488, we find a three-line lament (one of the numerous formally recognised topics that also included the seasons, love, travel, habitations etc.) by the poet Sōchō on his former home and the people he had known in the past:

All I saw were sad
reminders of my old home
and people I knew

which is followed by this thematically linked two-line contribution by Sōgi:

Looking ahead to old age
what then can I rely on?

and in turn answered with a three-line response from a third poet:

These verses of mine
themselves just as colourless
may give me solace (Shōhaku)

The image of the greyness of old age is matched by the 'colourless' verses that will serve for companionship. But perhaps the deeper meaning is that neither old age nor poetry are really so colourless, but simply reflect the changes of life's seasons. We should not look for permanence.

Things come and go, and we can't 'own' them. Sōgi, the Zen Buddhist monk, says in another poem, using the image of reflected moonlight:

The ruling principle is
things come about on their own

water does not think
it needs to offer the moon
lodging for the night

Poems usually took up either a seasonal theme (and every poet would instantly know which season was being depicted by the choice of conventional 'seasonal' words such as 'plum' or 'cherry blossom' for spring, 'moon' and 'frost' for autumn, 'snow' for winter) or an emotion – of love, a meeting, a parting, a journey (employing words such as 'waves', 'shore', 'boat', 'bridge'); of loss, regret, the passing of time; and, by associating feeling and image, evoke the ephemeral nature of both seasons and relationships:

The moon must be there
somewhere seen somewhere even
on this misty night (Shōhaku)

frost is covering the fields
autumn has come to an end (Sōchō)

and:

The nights have gone by
uselessly so long apart
and now it's autumn (Sōgi)

the wind blowing through the reeds
how it interrupts my dreams (Shōhaku)

The 'dreams' being dreams of his lover from whom he is separated during these 'useless nights', the wind recalling the autumn season.

We do not find the 'haiku', the three line opening of the 31 syllable poem, established as a verse form in its own right until much later, in the Edo period (1600-1868) – also known as the Tokugawa period or the 'early modern age' after the imperial court had moved to Edo, the modern day Tokyo – most notably in the work of the 17th century master Matsuo Bashō. And at this point we should perhaps explain the similar and confusing terms that frequently occur in the literature, *hokku* and *haikai*, alongside references to 'haiku'. The *hokku* is technically and formally the first three-line (17 syllable) component of the 31 syllable poem (the last two-line element is known as the *waki* and the whole may be referred to as a *waka*). *Haikai* is the generic term given to this type of linked verse composition. 'Haiku' is the later term attached to the independent 17 syllable unit. On the surface, the 'new' verse form does not appear to be very different from the component of the linked verse sequence that preceded it. But what we notice as the haiku becomes more widely taken up is that it moves away from the imperial court and its manners and mannerisms into everyday life, both in terms of its subject matter and its wider adoption by the samurai warrior class, monks, merchants and lay people of all rank, as a stand-alone verse form to express in the particular the universal experience of the fleeting, evanescent nature of experience itself. This early haiku by Arakida Moritake (1473-1549):

A fallen blossom
blown back to the bough I thought –
no, a butterfly!

as well as being an interesting observation in itself, at another level also refers to the philosophical principle that, just as a stream can't flow back up a hill, fallen blossom cannot return to the bough. Time passes, and what passes can't be recovered. The magic is that the haiku does just that by capturing the passing moment.

Japanese haiku and English versification

In the Japanese transcription of the haiku by Bashō we quoted earlier, it is noticeable that every word in the original version ends in a vowel. Japanese is a language with few consonants and a limited range of constantly recurring vowel sounds. It does not lend itself to the long, fluid or melodic line of, say, classical Greek or Latin poetry, Sanskrit sung verse, English romantic poetry or the rich sound world of Mallarmé in French. It has both short and slightly longer vowel sounds (the longer vowel is indicated in romanised transliteration by a macron: ō and ū) but does not possess diphthongs (the way 'bow' and 'arrow' trail off instead of being pronounced 'bō' and 'arrō' with an unmodified vowel quantity characteristic of English north country dialect); and we do not find clusters of consonants (think of the sound combinations of 'phth' and 'ngs' in the word 'diphthongs' and the mastery of lips, tongue and teeth in combination we need to achieve them). We would therefore call Japanese a syllabic language in which we hear the same sounds recurring in combination and the repetition of vowel word endings. One of the consequences for poetry of such frequent vowel endings is that rhyming is so incidental that its deliberate use would become tiresome.

Japanese verse has found its natural form in a sequence of 'lines' of either five or seven syllables, established in the earliest collection of poems, such as the *Man'yōshū*, and persisting into the modern era. Those underlying evenly stressed syllabic values differ from the natural speech rhythms of the English language which, where not purely iambic (an unstressed syllable followed by a stressed syllable), are variants of the iambic; the underlying rise and fall of English is iambic:

the underlying rise and fall of English is iambic...

To summarise, the 'natural' line of Japanese verse is founded on the frequency of vowel sounds in the language, formally restricted to five or seven syllables. The entire meaning of the line, and its imagery, must be contained within that line length. Some aspects of Japanese help to achieve that concision, but others, notably the highly inflected verb forms that can in themselves take up the whole line, *add* to the line length. There are no articles in Japanese, so the definite article 'the' and the indefinite article 'a', so frequent in English, necessary for clarity, and an aid to rhythmic regularity in the verse line, do not take up syllabic space in the haiku. The absence of the person, of who exactly is doing what in relation to whom, the 'I', 'he', 'it', 'they' personal pronouns which are often omitted, also helps to reduce the syllable count in Japanese, frequently and often quite deliberately creating ambiguity, which is one of the recurring features of the haiku. In English we strive for exactitude, deciding between the appropriateness of '*a* monkey' or '*the* monkey', making it clear who is the subject: 'I am sitting' rather than just 'sitting', and generally trying to avoid syntactical uncertainty. The shorter we make statements the more ambiguous they are likely to become. As William Empson has said, 'ambiguity is a phenomenon of compression'[1] – and we can find examples of that effect in English verse, such as in the compressed syntax of Gerard Manley Hopkins's poem *The Windhover*:

> *...in his riding/ Of the rolling level underneath him steady air, and striding/ High there...*

English is a very flexible language capable of clear and precise expression, with choices of word order, a rich vocabulary rooted in the early history of island invasion, and a wealth of idiomatic and metaphorical usages and allusions. We have the words 'royal' and 'regal', for example, derived from Latin via French, but also 'kingly' from its Teutonic root in the Old English word for king, 'cyning'. The choice of vocabulary, the sound values of consonants and the variability of stress and vowel length all lend advantages to English, though they present different types of challenges to the poet. Many translations of Japanese haiku are shorter than their originals. For example, this very

[1] William Empson, *Seven Types of Ambiguity*. London, Chatto & Windus, 3rd edition. 1953

famous poem by Bashō lends itself to extreme concision in English:

furuike ya
kawazu tobikomu
mizu no oto

translates literally as

An old pond
a frog leaps in!
Water-sound.

which we can further reduce to just six syllables:

Old pond
frog leaps in.
Plop!

So a fundamental question arises when we first put pen to paper to write our own haiku: Why am I tying myself to the strictures of a syllabic language so different from my own, and counting syllables instead of saying what I want to say as economically and effectively as I can? That is a perfectly legitimate question, and as soon as we attempt to answer it we realise that the form alone does not define the haiku.

We might think of it like this. The formal elements of the haiku in Japanese are the 5,7,5 syllable count of its three line structure, which acts as a formal constraint on the choice and order of words and imagery, and the associations and ambiguities condensed in them. But the formal structure of the poem is not the essence of the poem, but is like a little bamboo box, always made with the same skilful technique, to capture a singing cricket. The cricket is the essence, always singing within the limits of what the poem can make to contain it.

The art of the haiku

This simple haiku by Bashō, which we quoted at the beginning of the book, is among his most admired:

kareeda ni
karasu no tomarikeri
aki no kure

Its bare elements, without regard to syllabic structure, can be literally translated as:

On a bare branch   *CONRINGSS*
crows roosting
autumn dusk   *CONRUNRSS*

There is nothing much to it, yet it works by capturing that quality of *sabi*, 'loneliness', much admired by the Japanese. Bashō chooses not to open the poem with the seasonal setting – the season is autumn, the time early evening – but closes the verse with it to add, word by word, greater depth of feeling to the simple opening scene. First he introduces the bare branch, so we know we are in a desolate season. Then the crows, which we picture black against the sky, adding to the spare, bare quality of the image. The crows are roosting, indicating a closing down, a settling down at the end of the day. 'Autumn' deepens the imagery and 'dusk' takes us towards the sense of an ending. Nothing needs to be explained, for what the haiku aims for and achieves is to capture the universal in the particular, the enduring experience of being, in the fleeting moments that make up our experience. If this emphasis on loneliness seems perverse among social and sociable beings, we only need to remind ourselves that while we share our lives with others, our thoughts and feelings are our own, my experience is mine alone, and being 'alone' in the midst of life is the very nature of individual experience. All our reasons are predicated on experience, and all experience is derived from the concreteness of reality. The haiku does not usually state the poet's feelings explicitly. It is the images which are concrete, explicit: the mood arises out of them.

Chikamatsu (1653-1725) revealed the secret of this art, writing not in fact of the haiku but of the theatre: 'It is essential that one not say of a thing that "it is sad", but that it be sad of itself.'[1] In the drama, as we know from routine made-for-TV films and plays, the easy route to engaging the audience without requiring any effort on its part is to create characters whose personalities and motives are so obvious they seem to have been written down and pinned to their costumes, and to explain the action as it goes along and signal what is going to happen next. Modern popular fiction has the same features, and poets fall into the same populist trap by appealing to our sentiments in defining their subjects as sad, or unjust, or horrifying; memorable, or beautiful or joyful; so we are in no doubt that the poet is angry, or protesting, or shocked or enchanted; and

[1] Donald Keene, *Anthology of Japanese Literature*. New York, Grove Press. 1955

we know not only what the poet (or author or dramatist) thinks but what we too are supposed to think or feel.

To allow things 'to be sad in themselves' we must seek to objectify what is in fact a subjective feeling by removing the 'person' from the action, then finding the person, the subjective mood, in the object itself. To achieve this we have to treat words themselves as 'objects' and not simply see them as links in the chain of a sentence by which we explain ourselves.

Words are the concrete material of a poem, as wood and its hardness and its grain is the material of the carving, stone and its qualities the material of the sculpture, and paint and its properties the material of the painting. Wood and stone and paint possess qualities of their own and have a material resistance to the imposition of the will of the artist, and a work of art will look forced if the artist is not able also to work as though his hand and eye and imagination were an extension of the nature of the material of his art. The finished work will speak for itself, but will not explain itself. The poem, too, must speak for itself. 'Poetry,' said the modern American poet Richard Eberhart, 'gives most pleasure when only generally and not perfectly understood.' Like all forms of art the poem retains a certain mystery, and that mystery is connected to the material nature of the work, to the concrete, and not to an expression of meaning, otherwise all art would be philosophy.

The imagery of the poem is crafted from words. But words are shifty and deceptive objects, for they are not natural objects but mental constructions. They have changed and evolved over time, and continue to do so. They have a history. They have already been used – and misused – and co-opted to the purposes of human mentality, not simply to enable clear communication but to persuade, to move, to dissemble, to deceive. How could there be a single unequivocal certainty attached to words such as goodness, truth, beauty, love, justice? They have been used to represent so many differing shades of subjective feeling. If we introduce such words, which are by their very nature ambiguous, into a poem then we must know that we are dealing with abstract concepts – perfectly legitimate subjects for poetry – which are not the imagery of experience but the representation of our reflections on experience, and our thoughts have to explain themselves.

But concrete nouns are also unable to escape their history. It is a feature of Japanese poetry that the simplest of images may be associated in the poet's mind with a similar image in another poem, and one that another poet or reader is expected to recognise. One could hardly write of the spring, of cherry blossom, of the wind on the mountain, of the crow on the branch, without in some way recapitulating all that has gone before, both as common imagery and imagery common to a number of earlier classical instances referred to and deferred to. The *Minase sangin hyakuin* was written as a votive offering to the shrine at Minase dedicated to the former Retired Emperor Gotoba. Its opening 'spring' verse:

yukinagara
yamamoto kasumu
yūbe kana

In the midst of snow
haze low on the mountain.
Evening!

alludes to a famous poem submitted to a competition held by the Emperor Gotoba (traditionally evenings had been regarded as best in the autumn, and dawns best in the spring):

miwataseba
yamamoto kasumu
minasegawa
yūbe wa aki to
nani omoikemu

Gazing out at
haze low on the mountain
over Minase River.
How could I think
autumn the season for evenings?

That shared history of words and images is not of course confined to Japanese tradition. In English we may, for example, in searching for the right word and image, have a choice between the word 'wood' and the word 'forest'. There is something darker and more forbidding about the image of the forest, something primeval (we speak of the 'primeval forest' but rarely of a 'primeval wood'). It is a place to hunt – and to be hunted. To be lost in a forest is to be more lost than in a wood. The forest has associations with fairy tales, with Hansel and Gretel. It evokes the forest in myth and legend, and in the fiction of Tolkien. A wood is less threatening; it has the possibility of a path through it and a way out of it, unless it is a 'dark wood', which returns the image to the haunted corners of the child's imagination and the *selva oscura* of Dante on his journey to the underworld. We cannot use a word casually, for every word is rooted in its history and deeply implanted in the psyche, consciously or unconsciously. Literary associations are usually more consciously held. No poet could consider using the words 'west wind' without deferring to Shelley's line in 'Ode to the West Wind' or perhaps bringing to mind the anonymous early English lyric:

> *Western wind when wilt thou blow,*
> *The small rain down can rain?*
> *Christ, if my love were in my arms*
> *And I in my bed again!*

As soon as we mention flowers or blossoms nodding together or blowing in the wind, appearing to be in conversation, we are at once in the world of Mukai Kyorai (whose poem is translated later in this book), Shelley (the west wind) and Wordsworth (his nodding daffodils). Thus we may find ourselves working in both a Japanese and an English tradition when writing an 'original' haiku:

> *More disputation.*
> *In the garden cosmos blown*
> *by the western wind.*

Words are the hard intransigent material of the poem. Words are the representations of images and ideas and are therefore intrinsically subjective in the way that wood and stone are not. They are already shaped with meaning, and the history of that meaning will inevitably shape whatever new thing is made with them. But words are also in essence sounds, vocalisations of things and the meaning of things.

In contrast with the even syllabic character of Japanese words, words in English have both stressed and unstressed syllables, and words of a single syllable *become* stressed or unstressed when they are combined with other single syllable words. In this line:

        ′   ′   ′   ′

The boy stood on the burning deck

'the' in both instances is unstressed, as is the 'ing' ending of 'burning' and the word 'stood', with the stress given to the preposition 'on' to create the regular rhythm. If this were not an iambic line of verse but a remark, the stress might change in this way:

        ′   ′   ′   ′

The boy stood on the burning deck

The words invite stress, and the combination of words creates patterns of stress and, as in this example, more than one possible pattern or rhythmic scheme.

Consonants in English also create a greater variety of sounds and sound combinations. Attached to stressed or unstressed syllables, to strong or weak vowel sounds, and with their own innate sound values, they add further complexity to the choice and association of words in a line of verse. If we go back to our 'forest' and 'wood' example, we can add to the imagery and associated meanings the weight of the words' own physical quantities and qualities. 'Forest' has two syllables and the second is unstressed. That fact, plus the soft 'f' and the sibilant 's' and the weaker 't' sound compared with the harder 'd' sound of 'wood', makes 'forest' a more murmurous, susurrant word than 'wood'. 'Wood' is the sound of the axe falling.

So we have a number of considerations to keep in mind when exploring the structure of a haiku in English (and for that matter, any line of English verse) which overlap with considerations of the Japanese technique but also present different obstacles and suggest differing treatment when we come to put the words together:

1. The word and its image or idea and its associations.
2. Its inherent or accepted meaning.
3. The ambiguity of words as representations of images, ideas and meanings.
4. The strength, length, weakness and stress of vowel sounds.
5. The assonance or dissonance of words and word combinations.

These are the qualities and quantities of the material of the poem, but the poem itself is the ordering of words, and it is the order, the syntactical arrangement of words in a line or in a sequence of lines, that transcends its material elements.

The haiku poet attempts to capture the moment, the passing moment whose passing is the essence of that moment. The haiku always creates the sense of the transience of the moment, passing from one image to another, one evoking the other, one reconciled in the other, so that somehow that transience is its own sufficiency. We do not ask of a haiku what it is 'about'. It is about nothing beyond its own immediacy. That sense of the totality of the immediacy of experience is achieved by pivoting the imagery of the opening line with the imagery of the two closing lines (or that of the first two lines with the final closing line) in a way that reconciles the two images (which may be complementary but as often as not seem contradictory or unconnected). We are left with the feeling that 'this is it' and that there is nothing to say before or after experience.

'Pivot' is the right word to use here. The two halves of the haiku are balanced: one turns in relation to the other; there is a sense of movement, in time or space, between the two parts; and, more technically, a 'pivot' word is sometimes used to make that link – that is, the same word, or the same word that will bear more than one meaning, both ends the first section and begins the second. The Japanese language with its frequent homonyms permits this more easily than English.

tachiwakare
inaba no yama no
mine ni ouru
matsu to shi kikaba
ima kaerikon

In this poem by Ariwara no Yukihira (818-893) the 'pivot' word with which the final couplet commences is *matsu*, 'pine', which in Japanese means both 'pine tree' and 'to wait', just as the word 'pine' happens to carry two meanings in English. The sense of the verse is 'Though I am to part from you for the 'pines' of Mount Inaba (that 'wait' for me) if I hear that you 'pine' for me I shall return.' The word *matsu* occurs only once, but syntactically suggests multiple meanings. But to pun the word 'pine' in English to simultaneously act as both the noun and the verb, and with different meanings, would not only be technically difficult but probably a little ludicrous.

But we need not ignore the possibilities of verbal ambiguity altogether. If I were to write:

Lost on the mountain
and then in the mist taking
the path to your door

interpreted literally it means the poet was lost on the mountain in the mist but took the path that led to his lover's door. But since he was lost, does it mean that he inadvertently arrived at her door? Or did he 'mistake' the path or 'miss taking' the path altogether and remain lost in the mist? We manage to create some ambiguity, but is the means skilful or simply an error of judgment and taste? In English the pun is almost always used in a humorous context, and its humour is not always applauded. Rather than using the trick of a pun as a pivot, we can allow the ambiguity of meaning to emerge out of an unnatural line break or by dispensing with natural punctuation to create a sleight of hand transition from one idea to another. In my own translation of the poem I quoted above:

In the midst of snow
haze low on the mountain.
Evening!

I might have chosen to write:

In the midst of snow still
haze low on the mountain.
Evening!

to suggest, by adding the word 'still' to the first line, that though it is spring there is still snow on the mountain slopes, but also that the haze is still, it too not melting away.

In that moment between dream
and reality dawning

showers of petals
drifting by in the moonlight –
unearthly vision

In this *renga* by Shinkei (1406-1475), the poet wakes before dawn, the moon still in the sky, his mind drifting between dream and reality, and sees the colourless spring blossom drifting ghostly in the moonlight, itself a vision between the real and the unearthly. The idea of drifting is only suggested by the experience of waking from dreaming, but that idea is turned into reality with the drifting of the blossom. By ending the second line with 'dawning' we are able to capture the original Japanese meaning of 'the sky before dawn' as well as the idea that the reality now 'dawning' is as uncertain as a dream.

Haiku in Japanese often also employ a 'cutting' word, a word recognised as bringing the first section, or the whole sequence of three lines, to a close. Bashō frequently used both the word *kana*, which implies a sense of wonder (rather like the regularly occurring 'O' which begins so many lines of English verse) and the suffix *-keri*, a form of exclamation, as well as conclusively ending a line with a noun. There is no equivalent for these cutting or ending words in English. The same effect can be produced in a number of ways, including the controlled use of punctuation: a question mark as the equivalent of *kana* and an exclamation mark for *–keri*; ellipses to indicated a sentence completed but implying something still unfinished…. We can also employ a stressed vowel sound to end the line or isolate it from the next line.

In the poem below by Bashō, we can substitute an exclamation mark for the final suffix. The poem has a title, a head note, to give it the context:

'Regretting the passing of spring, looking out over the lake.'

Yuku haru o
Ōmi no hito to
oshimikeri

So the spring departs
with those I met at Ōmi.
Bitter to the end!

In the translation below of a haiku by Ogawa Fūbaku, *kana* can be replaced by 'How' to capture the sense of wonder.

Iriai no
ume no narikomu
hibiki kana

Evening temple bell.
How it goes on resounding
in the trembling plum.

The stressed end word 'bell' and the period create the natural pause at the end of the first line. The word 'plum' is also a stressed syllable, and brings the last line to a natural conclusion, helped also by the natural rhythmic pattern in English of an unstressed syllable followed by a stressed one in the words 'resounding in the trembling plum.' It works well enough to allow us to omit the period at the end of the first line if we wished, and to rely on the line arrangement to enforce the pause that naturally follows the stressed 'bell':

Evening temple bell
how it goes on resounding
in the trembling plum

The important point is that a well-constructed haiku will fall into two parts marked by a naturally occurring pause. And the ending will sound conclusive:

The moon slipping through
this vast thicket of bamboo.
A cuckoo calling. (Bashō)

Although the final syllable here is unstressed it is not un-expected because the line's regular rhythm predicts it. And the incidental occurrence of a rhymed ending to the sec-ond line reinforces the sense of a conclusion to the first two line section.

The effect of the pause is not only to separate the two sections, but to make a link between them – a pause for breath in expectation of a second image that will take us back to reconsider the first, for the concluding line does not move us away from the first lines, but takes us back to them. The shape of a haiku is not linear but circular.

Japanese haiku in the modern period

While haiku from Bashō onwards looked back to classi-
cal models and traditional themes, its practice was part of
a wider developing interest in a variety of arts, literature
and entertainment. As we move into the 'modern' period
of printing, woodblock art, puppet theatre and works of
fiction, we see the art of haiku taken up as a cultural pur-
suit by people from all classes, from samurai to merchants,
monks and self-made men. While it continued to dwell
on the main topics noted earlier of seasons, love, lamen-
tation, journeys and partings, those themes are treated in
more everyday and down to earth imagery and language,
sometimes with humour and sometimes with a degree of
vulgarity. We can watch that process unfold with exam-
ples, beginning with Bashō and his disciples and on into
the twentieth century.

In the evening
I'll fall asleep drunk where wild
pinks bloom among rocks. Bashō

In this winter rain
even the monkey it seems
could use a raincoat. Bashō

The raincoat, *komino*, is a straw raincoat, which Bashō
would have been wearing.

Ill on a journey.
In dreams I am running through
fields of withered grass. Bashō

Evening shower.
Standing looking out at it
a woman alone. Kikaku (1661-1707)

Dreaming I was stabbed –
it was real after all.
Bitten by a flea! Kikaku

White flowers nodding –
old white-haired frontier guards
getting together. Kyorai (1651-1704)

All right, I'm coming!
I say. But still he bangs it,
my snow-covered gate. Kyorai

Something makes a noise.
A scarecrow fallen over
there all by himself. Bonchō (d.1714)

A bat glances by.
The wife from across the street
gives me a quick look. Buson (1716-1783)

The first line in the original simply says there's a bat. From that we recreate the experience of its quick flight. Did that really happen? Did the woman across the way really give me that look? In English we can take advantage of the variant meanings of 'glance' to make the connection between the two events more apparent – but the deeper, unexpressed connection of the original is better.

After the petals
have fallen their ghost rises.
O, those peonies! Buson

The image of the peonies remains in the mind – where it always was!

Over the dishes
sound of a rat scampering.
O, how cold it is! Buson

In that old pond
the frog grows older
and leaves are falling. Buson

Buson of course is referring to the famous haiku of Bashō as he reflects on the passage of time.

In the 18th century emerged the first anthologies of (largely anonymous) haiku known as *senryū*, taking a comic, satirical or irreverent attitude towards everyday observations of people and life in town and country. These are just two examples, taken from the *Yanagidaru* anthology. The first one I have rendered in a free, non-regular form.

Workmen eating
scattering complaints
like crumbs.

Sandals made from straw
hung from the window for sale –
God only knows when.

Servants in wealthier households made straw sandals for sale and hung them hopefully by the window.

The following haiku is an irregular rendering of a famous poem by the Zen monk Ryōkan (1758-1831):

The thief left something
behind:
moon at my window.

In the twentieth century, under the influence of Western models, the scope of Japanese poetry has expanded enormously. Yet the practice of haiku has continued, albeit often challenging classical models and rigid formality. Here is a one-line verse by Ogiwara Seisensui (1884-1976). I have tried to capture some of the repetitive sonorities of the original by translating the 'crying' of the insects as 'singing'.

mushi naku naka ni mushi naku

An insect singing
singing among insects
singing.

The spirit of haiku

In this brief survey of the history of haiku we can see that the subjects taken up by haiku go beyond traditional, formalised encapsulations of seasonal themes and pick up seemingly ordinary, everyday personal experiences. Given the tendency to bypass the formal 5-7-5 syllabic structure, particularly in translation, we might ask: Why is a haiku still a haiku when it has freed itself from the formal strictures that define it? Whatever we do with the poem's rhythmic construction, it will remain brief and it will have two balanced elements or ideas in it. Although the last poem quoted above is given in a short single line it none the less contains two elements: that an insect is singing and that (each) insect is singing among other insects – suggesting that the assertion of individuality simply contributes to the whole, and that the whole, the evening droning of cicadas in the trees, for example, is but an individual asserting its presence. What at first seems a slight, and possibly unnecessary observation is in fact the seed of a potentially lifelong reflection on the nature of the individual, society, creativity, ephemerality. Every successful haiku has a hidden depth. It achieves that in the first instance by cutting out of the rolling, hardly noticed stream of thoughts and sensory perceptions something noticeable, something that seems worth catching as it passes, something stayed. It may seem like nothing – a woman seen looking out at the rain – yet it is something in particular. Something unstated lies beneath it, the unstated essence of the particular that we have somehow intuited has a more general significance. We might in fact redefine the haiku as the art of recognising the universal in the particular, of apprehending something enduring at the centre of transitory experience.

This quality in art, the intuition of what lies beneath, the unstated essence of something, in Japanese culture is known as *yūgen* – Arthur Waley describes it as 'the subtle as opposed to the obvious; the hint as opposed to the statement.'[1] We also find in the haiku what we might call the 'naturalness' of the nature of things observed or felt, the

[1] Arthur Waley, *The Noh Plays of Japan*. London, Unwin. 1921

sufficiency of things as they are in themselves, their 'formless spirit', known as *wabi* in Japanese; and *wabi sabi*, the beauty and sadness of the imperfect. While these reflections take us to the heart of Zen Buddhism and its close relationship to Japanese culture and the art of the haiku, we should remember that the 'unstated' lies also at the heart of all artistic creation, Eastern or Western, and that for the artist and the poet, in the words of Wallace Stevens, 'the imperfect is our paradise'.

We may note, as we read, the 'spirit' of the haiku everywhere: in the soliloquies of the Dorset writer T F Powys: *I have a terror of anything that is sound and whole. I love a broken roller left in a field...*[1]; in that strange little work by the German Hugo von Hofmannsthal[2]: *A watering-can, a harrow left abandoned in a field, a dog in the sun, a poor churchyard, a cripple, a small farmhouse, any one of these can become a vessel for my revelation*; and this sentence translated from the French of Colette: *During a sudden silence, thick as a mist, I've just heard fall on a nearby table the petals of a rose which also only waited to be alone before shedding its blossom.*[3] O, how that word 'also' transforms a statement of fact into an unfathomable mystery!

Nowhere do we find that spirit more readily than in the poetry of William Wordsworth. He writes in *The Prelude*:

> *There are in our existence spots of time,*
> *That with distinct pre-eminence retain*

[1] T F Powys, *Soliloquies of a Hermit.* Andrew Melrose. 1918

[2] Hugo von Hofmannsthal, *The Lord Chandos Letter.* 1902. Translated by Michael Hofmann and published by Penguin Books

[3] Colette, *The Evening Star.* London, Peter Owen. 1973

A renovating virtue, whence, depressed
By false opinion and contentious thought,
Or aught of heavier or more deadly weight,
In trivial occupations, and the round
Of ordinary intercourse, our minds
Are nourished and invisibly repaired...

We rescue the essence of experience from the common round and dead weight of our daily lives in the recollection of 'spots of time' in which the world seems to offer up in the moment something enduring that lies beneath its transitoriness in time. Just as with the image of the sound of the temple bell continuing to reverberate in the trembling plum blossom, or the peony that lives on in the mind after its petals have fallen, for Wordsworth the recollection of the imagery of cliffs and crags, lakes and mountains, trees and humble cottages, impressed upon his imagination in childhood, revivifies the dull round of life with the secret promise of eternity that the imagination finds in them: ... *they build up greatest things/ From least suggestions...* [2] In the following passage, for example, do we not find all the familiar elements and imagery of the classical Japanese haiku, and that same quality of something more *unstated*? He remembers that he had lain awake on a summer night

...to watch
The moon in splendour couched among the leaves
Of a tall ash, that near our cottage stood;
Had watched her with fixed eyes while to and fro

[1] Book 12, lines 208-215

[2] Book 14, lines 101-102

~ 39 ~

In the dark summit of the waving tree
She rocked with every impulse of the breeze.[1]

The poet lies in bed, the moon is similarly 'couched' in the leaves of the tree. His eyes are unwavering (the poet is the fixed point in this world of appearances) at the mysterious appearance of the moon rocking in the waving branches of the tree. Under other cultural circumstances could that experience have found its expression in the medium of the haiku?

SUMMER

Awake in my bed
I watched the moon in the tree
swaying in the breeze.

Writing your own haiku

It is time to begin to build up a few rules of engagement for the practice of writing haiku, and sketch out some provisional answers to some of the questions that commonly arise in the mind of the poet, before moving on to some practical exercises.

The first concerns the raw material that forms itself into the substance of the haiku. The haiku inhabits a world of concrete things in contrast to a world of abstract ideas. Whatever ideas or thoughts we abstract from the haiku arise out of the poem itself and not from statements embedded in the poem. The raw material of the haiku is the raw material of experience. We may, on the evidence of what we have said so far, divide experience into three cat-

[1] Book 4, lines 87-92

egories: direct, immediate experience; the recollection of experience; the experience of the imagination at work. We might classify as an example of direct experience the famous poem of Bashō already quoted:

Old pond
frog leaps in.
Plop!

But the haiku by Buson that is a consciously crafted allusion to it is a work of the imagination:

In that old pond
the frog grows older
and leaves are falling.

The haiku I have extracted from the verses by Wordsworth, quoted above, is an example of the recollection of an experience, one of those 'spots of time' that stay with us and reinvigorate our lives in dull times. The following haiku by Buson combines all three forms of experience: the actual, the piercing acuteness of the remembered past, and the construction of the imagination.

The frost is piercing.
In the bedroom I step on
my dead wife's comb.

No doubt Buson did step on his wife's comb in the bedroom, and he saw the possibility of linking the piercing cold to the piercing of his foot. And thence to the piercing memory of his late wife. But at the time he wrote the poem his wife was very much alive! So this was an imagined scenario designed to bring together those three connections very artfully and effectively. 'But it's not a true experience,' we may object. Certainly it may not be true in terms of *historical* time. None the less we are unable to deny it the truth of experience, of the concrete and particular made general and universal: a far more important form of truth than the veracity of isolated incidents as mere events. Poetry gives us truths that history is unable to discover among the thickets of lost experiences.

Some of the best translations of Japanese haiku don't follow the traditional syllabic pattern. So, should the writer of original haiku in English adhere to the 5,7,5 three-line form, or is there room for flexibility? All forms of verse have a structure. What came to be called 'free verse' in the Western world was a conscious move away from the restrictions of more formal traditional versification towards the rhythms of natural speech. Poets who led that movement, Ezra Pound for one, were fully competent in traditional verse forms such as the sonnet and the sestina and remained in complete control of the line and the shape of the free form poem. Poets, like painters, are advised to apprentice themselves to their masters and to the techniques of their art before forging original forms of expression. Even though there are precedents for variable line lengths in haiku in English, the beginner will benefit from mastering the traditional form. It is a good discipline. If your first attempts don't work then you are forced into rethinking the choice and order of words and the relationship between the two parts of the verse. Nor is it enough simply to achieve the right line length in terms of the syllabic count – the verse must sound perfectly natural and reflect the natural speech rhythms of the English language. Poems, wrote John Keats, should come naturally 'as the leaves to the tree' – or at least they should appear so and not show their working out. In striving for simplicity the striving should never be apparent. Here's a warning from the haiku poet Shiki (1867-1902):

Falling asleep
under the cherry blossom.
No need to work at it.

However, we should always beware of forcing the syllabic line length by adding extra words simply to meet that objective. If you have refined a haiku to the best of your ability and it seems to work even though it falls short of or overruns the line length, then don't mess with it.

One other note of caution: when running over a five syllable line into a seven syllable, or a seven syllable line into a five, you can't end the first line unnaturally, with an article or hanging preposition that really belongs on the next line, simply to achieve the right syllable count. Above I translated the haiku by Buson irregularly as:

In that old pond
the frog grows older
and leaves are falling.

To achieve regularity I might have tried to write:

In that old pond the
frog now is growing older
and leaves are falling.

The definite article at the end of the first line is a definite mistake, and lengthening the second line spoils the descending scale of the original, shorter line whose 'falling' rhythm continues into the last line and echoes the sense of its final word.

Do haiku need titles? Haiku have traditionally been anthologised by season or topic, and this practice makes the theme of each haiku more explicit – so we often see haiku with 'titles' such as 'Spring', 'Autumn' or 'Sorrow'. Many have specific titles such as 'Watching the moon go down' that provide a context for the poem. Many of the haiku of Bashō are set within a longer prose narrative, and others give a specific setting or quote a line from a well-known Japanese or Chinese verse as the topic. The title or introductory narrative, if you decide to employ this device, should not set out to 'explain' the poem, but to extend the 'moment' that gave rise to it or to set it in the context of a longer reflection that led to the haiku as a definitive statement into which those thoughts have been resolved.

A haiku works when the images work, when the juxtaposition of images 'says' what we think, feel, mean. But we must take care not to confuse 'images' with 'poetic imagery'. In the haiku two associated images are linked together, often quite subliminally, or enfolded one with the other. They are not *compared* in a simile. The echo of the temple bell is not 'like' the trembling of the plum blossom; they are *really* connected in a sort of synaesthesia of the senses, of sight and hearing. We would spoil the effect of

White flowers nodding –
old white-haired frontier guards
getting together.

by casting it more explicitly as a simile:

White flowers nodding –
like old white-haired frontier guards
getting together.

We should be able to turn in our mind from one image to another and let them reverberate, let them speak. The Imagist movement in poetry that emerged at the beginning of the twentieth century was a short-lived attempt to dispense with both classical and romantic fanciful imagery and make the concrete image the essence of the poem. Imagist poets were influenced by both Chinese poetry (and in particular by the Chinese ideograph held, if erroneously, to be a simpler, visual language of concrete imagery) and the Japanese haiku. But the short form proved restrictive to wider poetic needs, though the various manifestos and theories of the time would give rise to the main current of modern poetry led by, among others, Pound, William Carlos Williams, Marianne Moore, in which the concrete image and the natural 'breath' of the line would come to define the language of contemporary verse. But the Imagists did not always escape the simile. In the pioneering poems of T E Hulme, a good poet and a rewarding philosopher, still the 'ruddy moon' is *like* a 'red-faced farmer', sounds 'flutter' *like* 'bats in the dusk'. The simile has come to define the nature of what is considered 'poetic' nowadays. Poets search out similes, and similes within similes. 'This' is *like* 'that', and 'that' is *like* another image that comes to mind. If we were to remove the word 'like' from the vocabulary of poetry the larger part of contemporary verse would deflate *like* so many balloons. Similes work when one thing is *really* like another, and that other helps define the reality of the one. When Robert Frost in his narrative poem *The Witch of Coos* describes a skeleton *carrying itself* up a flight of stairs 'like a pile of dishes' we are astonished at the aptness of the simile, for the occurrence is so unusual that it *must* be 'like' something else. It is 'like' a pile of dishes because it not only carried itself up the stairs but carried itself 'from cellar to the kitchen', as though it had every right to it, like the dishes. The simile is essential. This simile in the *senryū* previously quoted also works:

> *Workmen eating*
> *scattering complaints*
> *like crumbs.*

It works because it conjures up the image of men talking and eating at the same time, scattering complaints and crumbs in one and the same reality. A contrived poetic simile such as 'lips like coral' is fanciful imagery unrelated to reality, not an image, and poetry's perpetual search for similes is in danger of carrying off our poeticising of the ordinary to extreme heights of absurdity. The following line once turned up in the (rejected) manuscript of a romantic novel: 'Their lips stuck together, like spaghetti sticks to the ceiling.' Beware of the simile!

Working with the material

Let us now look more closely at the act of creation. Haiku are, of course, written from the material of direct personal experience or reflection. If we are to tackle some exercises we need some material to work with, and for this purpose I have chosen to explore the sources of Wordsworth's famous short poem on daffodils, published under its first line title, 'I Wandered Lonely as a Cloud', and to see how we might draw on them to create haiku. If that seems a little irreverent, we have a number of 'permissions' to do that. We have Wordsworth's own preoccupation with 'spots of time', of which this recollection of a host of golden daffodils is one. The experience on which the poem was based is recorded in the journal of Dorothy Wordsworth for Thursday 15th April 1802. The first draft of the poem was not written until two years later, and was first published in 1807. The second, revised version with an additional stanza – the version we know from anthologies – was published in 1815. The poem was not a spontaneous response to immediate experience, but a carefully wrought later construction that may have been inspired by a reading of his sister Dorothy's journal entry, which we will be drawing on ourselves. Further, two lines of the poem – lines Wordsworth considered the 'two best lines' in the poem – were in fact contributed by his wife, Mary, and he was happy to acknowledge their source. The lines are:

They flash upon that inward eye
Which is the bliss of solitude;

The poem was the product of a common experience, a shared memory and a collaborative imagination in which we ourselves may vicariously participate. Below is an excerpt from the journal entry, followed by the standard published text of the four-stanza poem.

When we were in the woods beyond Gowbarrow park we
saw a few daffodils close to the water side, we fancied that

*the lake had floated the seeds ashore & that the little colony
had so sprung up - But as we went along there were more
& yet more & at last under the boughs of the trees, we saw
that there was a long belt of them along the shore, about the
breadth of a country turnpike road. I never saw daffodils so
beautiful they grew among the mossy stones about & about
them, some rested their heads upon these stones as on a pil-
low for weariness & the rest tossed & reeled & danced &
seemed as if they verily laughed with the wind that blew
upon them over the Lake, they looked so gay ever glancing
ever changing. This wind blew directly over the lake to them.
There was here & there a little knot & a few stragglers a
few yards higher up but they were so few as not to disturb
the simplicity & unity & life of that one busy highway. We
rested again & again. The Bays were stormy, & we heard
the waves at different distances and in the middle of the
water like the Sea. Rain came on...*

*I wandered lonely as a cloud
That floats on high o'er vales and hills,
When all at once I saw a crowd,
A host, of golden daffodils;
Beside the lake, beneath the trees,
Fluttering and dancing in the breeze.*

*Continuous as the stars that shine
And twinkle on the milky way,
They stretched in never-ending line
Along the margin of a bay:
Ten thousand saw I at a glance,
Tossing their heads in sprightly dance.*

The waves beside them danced; but they
Out-did the sparkling waves in glee:
A poet could not but be gay,
In such a jocund company:
I gazed—and gazed—but little thought
What wealth the show to me had brought:

For oft, when on my couch I lie
In vacant or in pensive mood,
They flash upon that inward eye
Which is the bliss of solitude;
And then my heart with pleasure fills,
And dances with the daffodils.

We can begin by making a list of the elements of the journal entry that look promising as the source of concrete images for haiku, and the thoughts and feelings they inspire.

1. A few daffodils by the waterside.
2. Some thoughts about how a colony may have arisen from seeds floated on shore.
3. Standing under the bough of a tree looking at a long belt of daffodils along the shore, comparing it to a turnpike road.
4. There is the sense of a journey in: *the simplicity & unity & life of that one busy highway. We rested again & again.*
5. Some flowers grew among mossy stones, where some rested their heads as though weary.
6. The rest tossed/reeled/danced/laughed, ever glancing and changing in the wind.
7. A stormy, windy day with waves surging on the lake, sounding like the sea.

How many of these elements did Wordsworth make use of, and how many more did he add from his imagination? Ignoring for the moment the second stanza, which he introduced in the later revision, in the first stanza he sets the location, *Beside the lake, beneath the trees*, and describes the daffodils as *Fluttering and dancing in the breeze*. The daffodils are a 'crowd', a 'host' and not a highway. In the third stanza he picks up the 'dancing' analogy again, the image of 'laughing' from the journal description (he replaced 'laughing' in an earlier version of line four with 'jocund'), and links the image of the sparkling waves on the shoreline with the 'gay' and 'glancing' movement of the flowers. But the central subject of the poem is *recollection* – the recollection of one of those 'spots of time' that bring the poet back to life from ennui, from a 'vacant and pensive mood', one in which the heart leaps and 'dances with the daffodils'. Wordsworth's 'two best lines' are truly the essence of the poem: the inward eye, the power to remember, imagine and reconstruct that is 'the bliss of solitude'.

It is clear from the journal description that Wordsworth was not 'wandering lonely as a cloud'. He was not alone, and it was a wild overcast day that does not conjure up the image of a single cloud floating above the hills and dales. The added simile of the cloud, as well as being useful for the rhyme, prefigures in its loneliness the solitary poet in his vacancy in the final stanza. Wordsworth added the second stanza in the final revision of the poem, and here introduced the image of the milky way. This is the 'turnpike road' turned heavenward, the highway of daffodils compared to the continuous band of twinkling stars. Neither the lonely cloud nor the shining stars are elements of the actual recollected experience, but poetic metaphors associated in the poet's imagination with the raw material of experience. That material, and the poet's imaginative reworking of it, provides us with some scope for a few attempts at haiku in tribute to it.

We may, for example, be struck by the image of daffodils resting their heads on mossy stones as though weary, and we may be reminded, even within the limits of the material we have so far quoted, of Bashō falling asleep where pinks bloom among rocks, and of the anonymous mediaeval poet weary of the winter weather, wishing to be back in his bed again. So we may decide to create something that associates the daffodils resting their heads with the wind and rain and our own weariness and begin with:

Bent against the wind
the daffodils...

The first line luckily has five syllables. By running over into the next line we associate the image directly and exclusively with the daffodils. But what we want here is to conjure up the image of the *poet* bent *against* the wind, and the daffodils bent *by* the wind. So I will isolate the first line by adding the period:

Bent against the wind.

The line now stands alone, ambiguously, uncertainly, to mean either or both the 'I' of this poem and the daffodils which will form the subject of the next two lines.

Bent against the wind.
Daffodils rest their heads
on mossy stones.

We are a syllable short on each line of the final couplet. We can change 'rest' to 'resting', the continuous present, which I think is better. And replace 'on' with 'among':

Bent against the wind.
Daffodils resting their heads
among mossy stones.

On second thoughts I don't like the clash of 'mong' with 'mo' of 'mossy' and prefer the definitiveness of 'on'. I can retain 'on' if I add the definite article before 'mossy' to get the syllable count right. Is that merely a filler word, or does it help with anchoring the image in the real and definite?

Bent against the wind.
Daffodils resting their heads
on the mossy stones.

Now we can see that what at first appears to be a very simple descriptive statement is built up from several layers of association. By using the word 'against' in the first line instead of 'by' we are not directly describing the daffodils bent by the wind. The daffodils have succumbed to the wind, they are bent back on themselves. Something else is struggling 'against' the wind, the poet, but the word 'bent' acts as a pivot to link poet and daffodils. One must persevere, the other is already able to rest, suggesting the poet, too, looks forward to resting. The stones are hard, the moss is soft. Out of this conjunction of images we are able to speak not simply of spring flowers but of the struggle of life against weariness, taking us back to the heart of Wordsworth's own poem and the image of the poet on his couch. Here is another haiku derived from the same material:

By the water's edge
daffodils. How few they are
in this sea of dreams.

We *imagine* that the seeds have drifted here across the lake (which in the wind sounds like the sea), and are reminded of the tentative nature of life, which is like a dream. Our moments are 'few' but those few moments are the seeds of our being, our renewal, our spring. We might have set the context of this verse with a header note, in the Japanese tradition, taking the text directly from the journal entry:

SPRING

When we were in the woods beyond Gowbarrow park we saw a few daffodils close to the water side, we fancied that the lake had floated the seeds ashore and that the little colony had so sprung up.

By the water's edge
daffodils. How few they are
in this sea of dreams.

Here is another sequence using the same source:

Along the lake shore
spring has made a broad highway:
golden daffodils.

A banner of stars above
now that the clouds have dispersed.

Do you remember
how they seemed to laugh and dance?
wind blown spring flowers.

The first haiku in this sequence simply expresses the delight and surprise of discovering a long belt of daffodils, a broad turnpike road along a pathless shore. To introduce the association with the milky way, the haiku is answered with a couplet of fourteen syllables to create a *tanka*. The dispersion of the clouds after the storm evokes the image of the lonely cloud and reminds us of the poet's solitariness and how his heart 'dances with the daffodils'. That in turn leads to the 'recollection' of the sight of the daffodils and how, in Wordsworth's poem, which we can never divorce from the reuse of the original source material, however fictive, the recreation of that incident in imagination is the bliss of his solitude.

Travelling, resting,
watching the busy highway.
Daffodils nodding.

Here we are able to draw a parallel with the 'white flowers nodding' of the haiku by Kyorai, and if we have that in mind we will think of the daffodils in whispered conversation. We contrast the 'travelling' (wandering lonely as a cloud) and the 'resting' (out of the storm and the travails of the journey) with the busyness of the daily life of others, knowing that the memory of this sight will bring the poet back to life, the life of the imagination, in times when he, too, is too occupied with the mundane business of living.

SOME OTHER LEAVES:
SIXTY HAIKU AND SHORT POEMS

In this collection of original and translated haiku, divided into five sections of twelve poems, the first twelve are haiku or *senryu* in which I observe the traditional 5,7,5 format. In the next twelve the number of syllables or the line arrangement varies. The third division groups together twelve short poems which owe their existence to the influence of haiku and *tanka* forms. These are followed by a selection from the haiku of the Monk Ryōkan and a further twelve poems which are personal variations on themes by Ryōkan. Some have contextual notes. They are by no means 'perfect' haiku, but I share them to illustrate the scope available to us as we read, write, think and reflect on our poetic heritage.

12 HAIKU (regular)

Yellow sun blue sky
above and below the same
yellow field blue hills.

Spring. Lost in the woods.
White wild garlic and bluebells.
A lone pink flower.

She in her men's jeans
he his hair pinned up behind
seeking India.

One morning, in the garden of the hotel where I was staying in Mysore, a deeply autistic young girl was wandering under the trees, reaching out and touching the leaves. I spoke to her but she could not speak, though she smiled back. I asked her father if she was happy. Yes, he said, but she can't express her heart.

Happy inwardly
'but she can't express her heart'.
Lost in my own thoughts.

Holding a gnarled stick
an old woman in the wood
walking step by step.

Flock of sheep, blue rumps,
woolly clouds graze overhead,
remnants of blue sky.

As a boy I wandered in the public library day after day wondering whether I should spend my life among books or perhaps go to sea and have adventures. How did it turn out?

I lived among books.
Sometimes I thought of the sea
and a ship's siren.

Perhaps I am lost
perhaps I am waiting for
myself in the mist.

She lives her life – but
I know the taste of her lips
better than she does.

In the undergrowth
the corpse of a headless toad.
Ah, now it is known!

Two further reminiscences of a northern boyhood:

A long wait at night.
On the bus, cold chromium –
distant hill-town lights.

Beneath the gaslight
my grandmother sits and waits
for her dead husband.

12 MORE HAIKU (irregular)

The fairytale turret
where she listened and dreamed
is now a lumber room.

The present moment
ebbs away colourless.
The drone of engines passing.

The crows are around somewhere
but not in their nests
wrecked by wind and rain.

Under the ice
the fish are hidden
even from themselves.

A sudden flight of birds always for me disperses the weight of thought or preoccupation. This haiku in fact has seventeen syllables, but an alternative line arrangement:

Whatever it was
I was thinking of
vanished.
Full moon
flight of swans.

The next haiku, too, has seventeen syllables but is differently arranged – following a 7,5,5 syllable pattern. The mood is similar to the haiku above. Waking very early one morning in Africa, I found the man who was sweeping leaves last night was out sweeping leaves. It suddenly occurred to me that the anxiety associated with working and making a living comes about from dividing our lives into periods of work/not work – what is fashionably called work-life balance in our therapeutic times – but there is another way to look at time, which has no meaning for birds

or animals, is therefore not a burden and does not 'pass' in
anxiety over its passing.

*The cow that grazes
grazes.
The man who sweeps leaves
is out sweeping leaves.*

*Clouds drift in the water.
Suddenly a fish jumps
out of a blue sky.*

*Robins are puffed out
against the cold.
Well-fed cats stroll by.*

*My hand trailing
in the water.
The frog and I
surprise each other.*

*Small brown leaves
are blown from tree to tree —
sometimes one is a wren.*

*Last flower,
late bee.
Where now?*

*This is all a poet achieves
windfall fruit
some other leaves.*

12 SHORT POEMS

After many years
we speak hesitantly of the past
wondering if there is something
to forgive.

In the field of rape
yellow butterflies
are invisible.
Me?
I'm just passing by.

At the side of the road
molehills
their northern slopes
covered with snow.

There is no resurrecting
the common yellow
the common white
flat out under the tree.
They've been through
one metamorphosis
already.
Here's another.

Enough of this
alone in the dark
listening to the rain
thinking
of her warm knees.

Ice and snow
slow down
impetuous thoughts.
One
has to think
one
step at a time.

A mother to a sullen child:
We have too much to do
for you to enjoy yourself
battling alien invaders.

Lapwing rising
from the fields
cross the frame
of the window
and everyone
stops to look.

Until the mist clears
the church and its steeple
are suspended
between earth and sky.

They are up from the valleys
to look and to wish
sharing small change
for the bus fare home.

The grapes are ripe
on the trellis
by the window.
The birds are here
as usual leaving
wine-coloured doodles
for me to admire.

While you were working
the apple blossom fell one day
in a shower and apples
grew into their colours.
Here they are in a bowl.

12 HAIKU BY THE ZEN MONK RYŌKAN

New pond.
A frog leaps in
soundlessly.

Full moon.
In my garden
measuring myself against Bashō

Note: Bashō is the name of the tree as well as the poet.

Cherry blossoms falling
not falling
falling.

Someone visiting
again obliged
to take off my hat.

Summer night
counting fleas
until dawn.

Summer breeze
white peony petal
blown into my bowl.

In the hedge
fledglings
and morning snow.

The wind blows
fallen leaves
enough for a fire.

Evening cool.
Enough rice for tomorrow
in my bowl.

Maple leaves
first one side then another
falling.

All around me
the world
is cherry blossom.

Who will listen
to my sad tale?
Autumn ending.

12 POEMS INSPIRED BY THE POETRY OF RYŌKAN

Ryōkan evoked a memory of a boy's old-fashioned haircut, perhaps having his own hair cut or tied. Violets were flowering. When I was a boy my mother insisted on parting my hair on the left, though it naturally parted on the right. Just as coats button from the left for boys and from the right for girls, the same old-fashioned tradition was enforced for hair styles. The hair struggled to stay in place, and I, too, struggled, as I always have, against rules. In the spring, a bunch of tulips thrust into an old jam jar after a few days will wilt, and writhe in a tangle of stalks.

Your hair parts this side
Mother said though it struggles.
Tulips in a jar.

An open window.
I look out on the moment
but the past drifts in.

In that bad winter
snow and ice
on my chair and bed.

Buttercups and daisies
up to my chin
until it was time to go home.

Everyone tells me
go now if you want to see
the orange blossom.

Rain endlessly falling.
Sitting quietly
doing nothing.

High in her attic room
we talk until dawn
of what the years will bring.

River in winter.
A kestrel hugged to itself
waiting for the mist to clear.

These are bitter torrents.
All night the rain has cut us off
from yesterday and tomorrow.

I'm an old man now
and dream too easily.
Something remains unfinished
but not the last bottle of wine.

It's easy to talk
but the more you say
the more of what you say
will be untrue.

I leave you
all my worldly possessions
flowers in spring
summer swallows
maple leaves
the white unwritten snow...

FURTHER READING

Traditional Japanese Poetry (Star translated with an introduction and ven D Carter, is a fine anthology of the earliest times to the twentieth century and includ generous selection of haiku. Hiroaki Sato and Burton Watson's **From the Country of Eight Islands** (University of Washington Press) is also an excellent comprehensive anthology. **The Penguin Book of Japanese Verse** by Geoffrey Bownas and Anthony Thwaite, too, can be recommended. And no one should be without the two collections of Kenneth Rexroth, **One Hundred Poems from the Japanese** and **One Hundred More Poems from the Japanese** published by New Directions. The monumental collection of haiku by R H Blyth is the standard work, published by Hokuseido in four volumes: **Eastern Culture**, **Spring**, **Summer-Autumn**, **Autumn-Winter**. Blyth also published a number of works on *senryu*. His **Zen in English Literature and Oriental Classics** is also worth tracking down. Many of Blyth's books are now quite hard to find and expensive. The chapter *Zen in Haiku* by D T Suzuki in his **Zen and Japanese Culture** is also very useful for understanding the cultural and philosophical context of haiku. **The Monkey's Straw Raincoat** (Princeton University Press) is an important and scholarly translation by Earl Miner and Hiroko Odagiri of the poetry of Bashō and his followers. **Bashō: The Narrow Road to the Deep North** by Nobuyuki Yuasa (Penguin) is indispensable. Tom Lowenstein is a very fine translator who has published a beautifully produced book, **Classic Haiku** (Duncan Baird), collecting together some of the best work

Bashō, Buson, Issa and Shiki, with photographs by John Cleare. Harold G Henderson published his excellent **An Introduction to Haiku** in 1958 (Doubleday Anchor). It is probably still the best guide to the art of *reading* haiku, with some 375 rhymed verse translations of haiku by the same classic masters as those represented in Lowenstein's collection, with a generous selection from lesser known contemporaries. Buson's haiku have been translated by W S Merwin in **Collected Haiku of Yosa Buson** (Copper Canyon Press).

CPSIA information can be obtained
at www.ICGtesting.com
Printed in the USA
LVOW12s1936060318
568839LV00028B/3/P